CW01573446

Original title:
The Spirit of Giving Thanks

Copyright © 2024 Creative Arts Management OÜ
All rights reserved.

Author: Levi Montgomery
ISBN HARDBACK: 978-9916-94-354-0
ISBN PAPERBACK: 978-9916-94-355-7

The Softest Glow of Gratitude

When life gives you lemons, make a pie,
A smile and a wink, oh my!
Thank the clouds for shadows cast,
And giggle as they flutter past.

The sunbeams dance on muddy shoes,
In gratitude for all we choose.
A friendly cat might steal your chair,
But it's just his way to show he cares.

Hand in Hand with Thankfulness

With a skip and a hop, we share our cheer,
Trade socks with friends, how odd, my dear!
A pie made of laughter, a sprinkle of fun,
We gather together, basking in one!

High-fives with sprinkles, silly hats worn,
Our hearts like balloons, impossibly swollen.
With a wink and a chuckle, we pass the feast,
In this joyful chaos, we are all released.

The Gift of Presence

Unwrapping laughter, the greatest delight,
Your quirky dance moves, quite the sight!
A pinch of gratitude with every tease,
Friends gathered round, sharing with ease.

No gift wraps needed, just love in the air,
A sweater too tight? We giggle, we care.
Belly laughs echo, we're all in sync,
With hugs that squeeze harder than a kitchen sink!

Chrysanthemums of Appreciation

In a garden of giggles, blooms brightly today,
Chrysanthemums wink, come out and play!
With a quirky dance on the grass, we trot,
Thankfulness blooms in the silliest spot.

Raindrops like confetti, sprinkle delight,
As we leap through puddles, oh what a sight!
The big hugs are squishy, the smiles so wide,
In this comedy fest, let joy be our guide!

Whispers of Appreciation

A turtle thanked a snail for speed,
While sipping on a stinky weed.
He said, 'Your shell provides a ride!'
But snails prefer to crawl with pride.

With gratitude, we laugh and cheer,
For wobbly turkeys roaming near.
They strut and dance, all huff and bluff,
Thankfulness is quite absurd and tough.

A Tapestry of Thankfulness

A cat gave thanks for a sunny spot,
While plotting ways to catch the pot.
The goldfish swam in circles tight,
Said, 'Thanks for letting me see the light!'

The chicken clucked, 'I love this bread!'
But then she dreamed of beds instead.
A loaf appeared, a monster rare,
Giggles flew through the kitchen air.

Bounty of the Heart

A pumpkin said to an old corn stalk,
'You’re the best! Let’s dance and talk.'
The corn replied with a wiggle and shake,
'Just don’t step on my buttery flake.'

With pies and hugs, the party grew,
Each veggie shared their best debut.
The beans all cheered, 'Let’s raise a toast!'
For food, my friends, we love the most!

Echoes of Gratitude

A mouse tipped his hat to a big ol' cheese,
Said, 'You're the reason for my deep unease!'
But cheese just grinned, enjoying the fuss,
'They thank me too, but I'm still odd, thus.'

While birds chirped songs in high-pitched glee,
They thanked the worms for fancy trees.
A square dance broke out, full of delight,
In thanks and laughter, they danced all night.

A Gratitude Garden

In the garden where smiles grow wide,
We plant our wishes, side by side.
Each row a giggle, a chuckle here,
Harvest of joy for all that's dear.

We water the plants with a splash of glee,
Pull weeds of worry, let laughter be.
Every bloom's a jest, a pun, a quirk,
In this patch of humor where grins do work.

Sunshine beams bring warmth, oh what a treat,
As daisies dance to our silly beat.
The carrots wear hats, the peas tell jokes,
Nature's comedy, it pokes and pokes.

So come to our garden, bring your cheer,
There's plenty of joy for everyone here.
Together we'll grow this funny land,
Where the harvest of laughs is truly grand.

Gathering Blooms of Thanks

In a field of chuckles, we gather cheer,
With daisies of gratitude, oh so near.
Each petal whispers a joke so bright,
As we toil with laughter from morning to night.

Bright blooms invite us, ‘Come take a seat,
The sun’s having tea, and it’s really sweet.’
Tulips are giggling, the roses in stitches,
While the daisies tease with their funny glitches.

We toss in our thanks like seeds in a row,
Water them lightly with a goodhearted glow.
Who knew appreciation could tickle so much?
In this garden of laughs, we’re all in the clutch.

With buckets of humor and shovels of glee,
We dig up the treasures of kindness, you see.
Blooming together, a marvelous crew,
Gathering giggles, as flowers still grow.

Threads Woven with Kindness

In a quilt of laughter, each stitch a delight,
We weave our thanks with a thread of light.
Every knot is a chuckle, every patch a cheer,
As we gather our blessings, all cozy here.

Fuzzy and bright, our fabric of fun,
A patchwork of smiles, oh, we've just begun.
With a tangle of puns and a twist of grace,
We stitch up the moments, our happy place.

The yarn of goodwill, it tangles with ease,
Creating a tapestry of giggles and tease.
Here's a square shaped like a wiggly dance,
And another that tells of a clumsy romance.

So come grab your needle, let's fold in some cheer,
We'll sew up our laughter, no room for a sneer.
As each thread weaves kindness, a funny refrain,
Our quilt of gratitude will keep us entertained.

Gratitude's Gentle Whisper

When the dog steals my socks,
I smile instead of frown.
His tail's wagging with glee,
A thief in our town.

Each pancake flipped with care,
Flour dust dances in air.
My cat eyes it like gold,
Should I really be scared?

Thanksgiving hugs from my chair,
As the turkey gives a glare.
It’s not my kind of feast,
But hey, I won't share!

So here’s to all the laughs,
And the food that we munch.
With a side of good humor,
And a big pumpkin crunch!

Harvest of Heartfelt Joy

I planted seeds of delight,
They sprouted into giggles.
Carrots grew with pure glee,
Now they dance and wiggle.

My neighbor's pie smells so great,
I sneak in for a slice,
He turns and shouts for joy,
Sweets come with a price!

Gather 'round for the feast,
With hats made of corn husks.
We'll laugh till we can't breathe,
In our hilarious busks.

With spoons stirring up cheer,
And laughter in the air,
Grateful for these moments,
A little love and flair!

Echoes of Appreciation

Every sock that I lose,
Turns up as a prize.
My house is a treasure,
In a sock-hiding disguise.

The turkey wears a grin,
As we pile on the plates.
Being thankful's a treat,
Till the fridge fills with crates.

The kids are all in charge,
With pies stacked way too high.
One fell and hit the floor,
We all giggled, oh my!

Let's toast to the blunders,
Of our wild festive year.
For love and laughter shared,
Makes the best time of year!

Embracing Abundance

I made a grand charade,
With veggies carved with flair.
They squabble every year,
Does a pumpkin really care?

Cousin Joe brings his dance moves,
That make the table shake.
We spill drinks and then laugh,
At the mess that we make.

Gather 'round for good fun,
With laughter ringing loud.
In gratitude for mishaps,
We celebrate, so proud.

So here’s to bizarre moments,
That fill our hearts with cheer.
Thankful for the crazy,
That bring us all right here!

In the Warmth of Kindness

A pie on the counter, who knows how it came?
Maybe the neighbor, or the cat's wild aim.
We gather the goodies, we can't let it rot,
Laughing and munching, who brought what, we forgot.

Hands full of cookies, their crumbs on the floor,
We dance like we're kids, but we're not kids anymore.
With every small bite, giggles rise to the roof,
Admiring the chaos, that's our little proof.

Gratitude flows, mixed with whipped cream delight,
Each portion a treasure, seasoned just right.
We're full of good cheer, and oh, what a sight!
In a kitchen of kindness, the laughter takes flight.

Gathering of Grateful Souls

We gather 'round tables, for favorites galore,
The turkey does a jig, oh, it’s hard to ignore.
While Auntie's storytelling keeps stretching the night,
Uncle Joe's dad jokes—both a blessing and fright.

With glasses raised high, mimicking fine wine,
Toasting to memories, and margarine designs.
We may disagree on the best casserole dish,
But we all share a laugh, isn’t that the best wish?

A feast so divine, each mouthful a dream,
We’re rolling with laughter, bursting at the seam.
In the chaos of kindness, we clink and we cheer,
This gathering is priceless, and so glad you’re here!

Moments of Reflection

Reflecting on moments, both big and quite small,
Remembering the time when I tripped at the ball.
I laughed in my fall, with a hand on my knee,
“Good thing I’m not fragile!”—oh, what a sight to see!

Gratefully awkward, we find joy in the mist,
And pieced together laughter, you surely can’t resist.
We count all our blessings, however absurd,
'Cause a life filled with giggles is just what we heard.

So here’s to the memories, the mess and the glee,
The quirks of our family, wild and carefree.
We cherish the moments, the fun and the flair,
In a world full of chaos, we choose to just share!

Threads of Thankfulness

We weave together moments, like yarn on a spool,
Spinning tales of laughter, where nobody's a fool.
Each stitch telling stories, with a wink and a grin,
A tapestry of jokes, let's dig right in!

Thankfulness wrapped in a knot of delight,
Every thread is a giggle, pulling tight through the night.
We pull at the seams, oh, look at that tear,
"Should we mend that?" "Nah!"—more fun in the air!

Each patch has a purpose, with flavors so sweet,
From handshakes to hugs, we're light on our feet.
In this fabric of joy, we find our own space,
Together we're woven, with humor and grace.

Mosaics of Blessings

In the kitchen, chaos reigns,
Turkey's doing a little dance,
Cranberries bouncing off the walls,
Who knew they'd take a chance?

A table set for twenty-four,
But two forgot to RSVP,
Grandma's pie is mostly air,
And Uncle Joe's still stuck in a tree.

With laughter spilling like the gravy,
A toast to Auntie's burnt soufflé,
"We're grateful for what we just ate!"
As folks politely look away.

So let's raise a glass and cheer,
To friends who make us grin,
This buffet's a mosaic of joy,
Just don't ask where we've been!

The Calm After the Thankful Storm.

The dinner's done, the plates all piled,
Napkins tossed like confetti wild,
Chaos ruled, we ate our fill,
Now scattered crumbs mark the thrill.

Chairs askew, one's lost its leg,
Thermostats broke, the food's a keg,
Uncle Fred fell asleep on the pie,
While Aunt Sue tried to fly by.

Just hours ago, it was mayhem,
Now one fat cat's in the mayhem,
Elbows stuck to counters too,
While leftovers jive in a tasty stew.

So here's to the peace that comes post-meal,
To cluttered kitchens and fast wheels,
Next year we promise a better show,
But until then, bring on the dough!

Gratitude’s Embrace

Dear couch, you’ve borne my weight,
Through all this feasting and my plate,
I thank you for the fuzz you share,
And for hiding crumbs beyond compare.

My pants complain, they whispered loud,
As I joined the ravenous crowd,
But with every bite, I’ve realized,
The best part’s in laughter disguised.

From pumpkin spices to squashed green beans,
Oh how it feels like culinary dreams,
With every awkward Grandma hug,
And the dog that’s sniffing every mug.

Together we shared and bolted through,
Our rambunctious love, we always knew,
So here’s to the quirks we can’t dismiss,
In our crazy feast, we find pure bliss!

Harvest Moon Reflections

Under the moon, we give a cheer,
For all that's here and all that's near,
Our plates were full, our hearts aglow,
But really, where did that pie go?

Thankful for laughs, even the flops,
Like when Grandma dropped all the chops,
With forks a-flying and giggles shared,
We looked at the mess and just declared.

In the glow of candlelight's tease,
We thank the stars and gather ease,
To every misstep and lopsided cake,
In this great feast, it's fun we make!

So let's raise our mugs and toast our glee,
For family chaos and pumpkin spree,
Harvesting joy in every bite,
Under the moon, everything's right!

Celebrating Simple Blessings

A squirrel stared down from a tree,
Holding acorns like they'd win a spree.
I waved to him as if he could hear,
But he just flipped a nut, oh dear!

The neighbor's cat sang opera at night,
While my dog howled, what a fright!
We both joined in a wild duet,
A concert hall, without a vet!

Leftover pizza, a gourmet feast,
Paired with soda for a tasty beast.
Dance moves in the kitchen like pros,
While crumbs rain down on our toes!

A pumpkin pie with extra whipped cream,
Turns any dull day into a dream.
Together we'll toast with our mugs in hand,
To silly moments that life has planned!

Threading Thankfulness Through Life

A knitting club with laughter and yarn,
Each stitch a giggle, escaping the scorn.
Scarves so long they trip on the floor,
Styled as fashion, we just want more!

At work, we pass around the snacks,
Muffins and cookies bring no lack.
But when the last bite disappears fast,
Suddenly, friendships are unsurpassed!

Waking up to socks that mismatch,
Is just one way our mornings catch.
Each silly moment creates a laugh,
Turning our woes into a gaffe!

Finding joy in the broken chair,
Laughing that life could be so unfair.
We raise our cups to blunders galore,
In every flub, there's room to adore!

Radiance of Grateful Hearts

A flower pot with weeds in bloom,
We wonder how they found their room.
They dance in sunlight, quite the sight,
Making even gardeners take flight!

Grandma's hat, a sight to see,
She wears it proudly, full of glee.
While we giggle at her colorful flair,
She claims it brings joy everywhere!

A dog’s outfit, matching shoes,
He struts his stuff, loving the views.
But chasing a squirrel, what a fool,
Those outfits don't make him so cool!

In bonfire light, we roast some marshmallows,
Jokes about sticks turn us into shallows.
With laughter ringing under the trees,
Our hearts grow light like a gentle breeze!

Thankful Echoes in the Wind

Leaves falling like they've lost a race,
Dance around at their own quick pace.
I catch one with hopes to impress,
But it lands on my nose, what a mess!

Sounds of laughter in the great outdoors,
We chase our children, from house to stores.
They hide behind bushes, giggling loud,
In this chaos, we're always proud!

Baking cookies with a pinch of cheer,
We taste-test dough; oh dear, oh dear!
These culinary arts go awry,
Who knew a cake could fly so high?

A mishap here, with a playful pun,
Our lives full of joy; together we run.
In every giggle, we find our grace,
Finding warmth in this quirky race!

Echoes of Kindred Spirits

In a land where oversharing thrives,
We thank our friends for pizza dives.
With every slice, a laugh we share,
Sending love like floating air.

Cards with puppies, all the rage,
Funny memes on every page.
In gratitude, we leave no stone,
Except the one that's still not grown.

At family feasts, we tell tall tales,
Of burnt dishes and runaway snails.
A toast with soda, laughter loud,
Here's to the moments that make us proud.

So raise a glass, let merriment flow,
We'll dance like dorks, even in snow.
Together we shine, a vibrant crew,
Thankful and goofy, that's how we do!

Thankful Footprints

Tiptoeing through a field of pies,
With whipped cream hugs and no goodbyes.
Each footprint left, a giggle shared,
For all the times that someone cared.

Grateful for socks that match in flair,
And quirky relatives who love to stare.
We fall and laugh, and roll on grass,
With every stumble, we raise a glass.

The pets all gather, eyes so wide,
Hoping for scraps, they won't abide.
Turkey bits tossed in the air,
Paws dancing, oh what a snare!

In this parade of messy art,
We weave our stories, each a part.
So join the fun, it's never late,
Together we sparkle, it's simply fate!

A Celebration of Gifts

Wrapped in laughter, boxes abound,
With socks and love, what a find!
Giggles erupt when bows go astray,
A cap with ear flaps, hurray for play!

Inside my gift, a bouquet of chaos,
Dancing robot, just for pathos.
Donations made in names quite funny,
To hope and heal, and spread some honey.

Mom finds a spoon that's kooky and bent,
Makes soup with joy, what a splendid event!
Each gift unwrapped, reveals a tale,
Of heartfelt wishes and silly fails.

So gather 'round, it's time to cheer,
For every gift that brings us near.
With giggles and hugs, we lift our cheer,
Celebrating gifts that make us dear!

Mosaic of Mirth

In a patchwork quilt of jolly faces,
We stitch our laughs in all the right places.
With thread of kindness, we weave our fate,
Each square a memory, oh how great!

The pie crust cracks, and chaos ensues,
As the dog chases crumbs and kids lose shoes.
With jokes in our pockets, laughter ignites,
A fiesta of fun on these cozy nights.

Thank the stars for friends who cheer,
And the odd gift of socks that appear.
In this canvas of love, we splash with glee,
Creating a picture, just you and me.

Through giggles and cheers, we tighten our bonds,
In a dance of absurdity, nobody yawns.
Let's celebrate the quirky way we live,
In this mosaic, so much joy to give!

Embracing Abundance

I'm grateful for the socks I own,
Though one always disappears, it's flown.
Here's to the pizza by the slice,
Each mouthful tastes like pure paradise.

Thank you for the coffee brewed,
A morning hug, a friend renewed.
When sharing crumbs is quite the jest,
I swear it's better than a feast of jest!

Oh, how my fridge sings with delight,
Leftovers dancing into the night.
For every snack that fills my day,
I offer smiles, come what may.

And if I trip on all this cheer,
My clumsiness just brings us near.
In each mishap, laughter's found,
A glorious chorus, joy unbound.

Heartstrings of Gratitude

A helpful hand that ties my shoes,
With knots so tight, I cannot lose.
Thankful for friends who make me laugh,
Even when they steal my half.

For every phone call, awkward pause,
I give a cheer with loud applause.
Sharing memes at 2 AM,
What a sight, I'm wrapped in them!

Thank you, world, for my silly cat,
Who steals my chair and thinks that's that.
With purrs and antics, she shows me flair,
A bundle of joy, beyond compare.

And every time I find a dime,
I dream of treats, oh what a crime!
Gratitude flows like rivers wide,
With laughter from my joyful side.

The Joy of Togetherness

Gather round for board games tonight,
Where losing is fun and laughter's in sight.
Each move's a giggle, a playful fight,
In the chaos, we find pure delight.

Thankful for friends who burn the stew,
We eat with joy, it's better than brew.
Our toast may flop, yes, it's true,
But taste of love shines right on through.

In every joke and silly pun,
We celebrate until the day is done.
With messy hair and sleepy eyes,
We count our blessings, no surprise.

Together in the dance of life,
Through every trouble and silly strife.
In every hug, every smile we share,
There's a kind warmth; it fills the air.

Thankful Leaves in Autumn

Oh, how the leaves dance in the breeze,
Thankful for nature's colorful tease.
Each crackling step on a bright red pile,
Reminds me to pause and just smile.

For pumpkins round and apple pie,
Delightful aromas that make me sigh.
When baking fails, I just improvise,
With a wink and a laugh, that’s my prize.

The furry hats in mornings so cold,
Wrap me in comfort, a hug to hold.
Grateful for warmth and light in my life,
Even if it means wearing my wife's — oh strife!

So here's to the quirks that make me swell,
In this harvest season, I surely dwell.
With every chuckle and joyous howl,
I give thanks with a happy growl!

Beyond the Mirror of Thanks

In a world where thanks are tossed,
I found a mirror, nearly lost.
It cracked with laughter, oh what a sight,
Reflecting joy, from morning to night.

With every nod and every grin,
It bounces back, where do I begin?
Gratitude dances in silly shoes,
Tickling funny bones, who knew you'd lose?

Underneath it all, a joke unfolds,
A turkey prancing, not feeling bold.
It winked at me, said, 'Don't you fret!'
Next year, I swear, I'm your pet!'

So here we stand, with cups held high,
To laugh and share, oh me, oh my!
As thanks go round, in quirky cheer,
We toast to life, and you, my dear!

The Colors of Appreciation

Red is for laughter, orange for fun,
Yellow is sunshine, where we’ve begun.
Green brings the giggles, blue lays the tease,
Together we dance, like a playful breeze.

A palette of smiles, splashed here and there,
Thanks painted boldly, with a humorous flair.
Every stroke whispers, 'Life's just a game!'
Who knew gratitude could be so insane?

In purple pajamas, we lounge and unwind,
Shouting sweet thanks, of the silliest kind.
With glitter and sparkles, we throw up our hands,
Let's celebrate wacky, in colorful bands!

So gather your friends in this art gallery,
We'll paint our blessings, with laughs, not a worry.
A canvas of joy, that's swirled and bright,
In the colors of love, we'll dance through the night!

Lanterns in the Dark

In the dark, lanterns sway,
Sending out thanks in a zany way.
Each flicker a chuckle, each glow a grin,
As we trip on laughter, let the fun begin!

Floating on wishes, like balloons in the sky,
We gather our giggles, oh me, oh my!
With each little lantern, a story to share,
Thanking the light in the night’s wild air.

They bobbed and wobbled, in a comical dance,
Each one a messenger, of a lucky chance.
So I'll shout thanks loud, until morning's glow,
For all of the quirks in the friends that I know.

Under this canopy, of giggly bright beams,
Let’s toast our oddities, and outrageous dreams.
With lanterns alight, we wander and roam,
In the dark, grateful laughter feels just like home!

Harmony of Hearts

Hearts beat together, in a funny parade,
Making a ruckus, a jubilant charade.
With thanks in our tummies, and giggles in line,
We march to the rhythm, in a conga divine.

A chorus of chuckles, a symphony loud,
Each beat a reminder, to thank our proud crowd.
With every tickle, and every wacky move,
We celebrate life, with gratitude groove.

In the rhythm of moments, the humor we find,
A dance of delight, perfectly aligned.
Oh, the joy we share, as we sing out our song,
In this kooky harmony, we all belong!

As we whirl and twirl, what a sight to see,
Hearts full of thanks, like honey from a bee.
In laughter we're bound, forever to part,
Singing our thanks, from the depth of our heart!

The Dance of Thankfulness

In the kitchen pots go clang,
As we try to sing and hang,
Grandma's pie, we hope is sweet,
Who knew thanks could taste like wheat?

Swinging forks like dancing feet,
Mouths are full, oh what a treat!
Siblings laugh, they spill their juice,
Thankful for this fun excuse.

Cousins trot around the floor,
Dancing like we've lost the score,
With turkey legs, we do a jig,
Who knew gratitude's so big?

In this chaos, joy ignites,
With each giggle, spirit bites,
So raise your cups, let's toast tonight,
For hearts and bellies feeling light!

Cherished Moments

Crafting memories with a smile,
Each silly story stretches a mile,
A burnt roast, it's charred and black,
Yet laughter's here, no need to snack.

Grandpa trips, the table shakes,
As we dodge the mashed potato flakes,
Thankfulness hangs in the air,
Mixed with giggles and a little flair.

From little kids with crumbs galore,
To grown-ups searching for the floor,
Each moment holds a quirky song,
In this chaos, where we belong.

So let's raise a glass of cheer,
For goofy times that draw us near,
In cherished moments, we all bask,
With laughter's light, we need not ask!

Endless Thanks

Oh, what’s this? A food-filled spree,
With pies and cakes, and jelly tea,
Belly grumbles start to hum,
But wait—who’s bringing in the drum?

A cat sings loudly on its chair,
While Uncle Joe gives us a scare,
Each bite's a joke, a tasty prank,
For all our treasures, we give thanks.

From veggies green to pudding’s shine,
Turkey winks, “I’m yours, not mine,”
As chaos reigns in this delight,
Gratitude giggles through the night.

In endless bites, we chew and talk,
Friends and family walk the walk,
Thankful hearts keep food in sight,
For every laugh, this feels just right!

Ripples of Kindness

A kind word floats like a breeze,
Tickling funny bones with ease,
Share a smile, it’s not too hard,
Let’s turn that frown into a card.

Pizza parties, laughter loud,
Friends gather in a joyful crowd,
With silly gifts that often break,
Each token brings a hug, not ache.

From neighbor’s pies to sister’s cheese,
In every bite, we find great peace,
Ripples swirl as kindness flows,
In each heart, that gratitude grows.

So let’s keep tossing kindness high,
Like confetti in a joyful sky,
With every laugh and tasty cheer,
Together we spread love far and near!

From Table to Heart

From the table, laughter rolls,
Past the turkey and the bowls,
With every giggle, joy ascends,
In this feast, the fun transcends.

Mashed potatoes in a fight,
Flying forks? What a sight!
With every spill, our hearts entwine,
In goofy moments, life's divine.

From Grandma's cookies, sweet and round,
To Uncle Dave, who can't be found,
This table's a stage, laughter's cast,
In humble meals, good times are vast.

So as we munch and chat away,
Thankful vibes come out to play,
From every plate, to every heart,
In this feast, together we start!

Gratitude's Gentle Dance

In socks that slip, we twirl around,
A dance so silly, none make a sound.
With breadsticks waving, we take a chance,
To thank the spaghetti with a goofy glance.

The cat joins in, a furry delight,
Batting at grapes with all of her might.
While grandma giggles, her pies on the floor,
She's thankful, I swear—who could ask for more?

We lift our glasses, cola in hand,
To everything mishap that we didn't plan.
Like face plants in mashed spuds, it's all in good fun,
We cheer for the chaos; hilarity's won!

So here's to the jokes, the laughter we share,
For life's goofy moments, we'll always prepare.
With hearts full of joy and our bellies quite round,
Gratitude dances, a whirl of profound.

Celebrating Small Miracles

Oh, the wonders that come from the tiniest things,
Like finding a sock that has all of its flings.
Spilled juice on the table? Just call it a chart,
Every sticky spill is a work of true art!

A dog with a wig, prancing around,
A miracle woven in laughter is found.
Each honk of the horn, each wacky surprise,
Scratches our heads, and brings tears to our eyes.

The sprout in the garden, a bean that will grow,
Celebrating the fact that we watered it slow.
A gnome with a grin, standing vigil with cheer,
We're thankful for him and the leaves showing here.

So toast to the mishaps, the sillies galore,
Bubbles of laughter—they're not a chore!
In small little miracles, life finds a way,
To dance in our hearts, and make quite the play.

Overflowing Bowls of Kindness

A bowl filled with cookies, oh what a sight,
But they vanished too fast; what a delightful fright!
Each bite brings a giggle, a crumb on the cheek,
Kindness is sweet, and it's the sugary peak!

A casserole bubbling, a chaotic stew,
With a pinch of mishaps and laughter, not few.
Grandpa's green jello—who knows what's inside?
A little surprise, but we'll take it with pride!

We gather 'round tables with laughter so loud,
To celebrate kindness and all that we've vowed.
With soup in our hair and good fortune on hand,
A feast for all senses, a joyful, wild band!

So let's raise a toast to the chaos we share,
To overflowing bowls and the love we declare.
With smiles all around, let this moment be grand,
In a world full of joy, let's take a firm stand.

The Warmth of a Thankful Heart

When pancakes flip and syrup does pour,
A breakfast ballet, who could ask for more?
With butter that slides and giggles that swell,
A morning to cherish, a story to tell!

A sunny side up, but the dog takes a dive,
And steals the whole plate—what a way to thrive!
Thankful for moments, both silly and bright,
Finding joy in the laughter, it just feels so right.

With puns in the air and smiles on our face,
A heart full of warmth, in this laughter, we race.
For every big blunder, we'll cheer with a roar,
Thankful in heart, for the fun we adore!

So gather your friends, let the laughter take flight,
With stories to share, we'll dance through the night.
In gratitude's glow, we'll embrace all the mirth,
For each silly moment, we celebrate worth!

Blessings Tucked in Every Corner

In the cupboard, snacks galore,
Forgotten chips, who could ask for more?
A sock that dances, one that sings,
Finding treasures, oh what joy it brings!

A cat that plots to steal my chair,
While cuddly dogs just sit and stare.
The garden gnomes, all dressed to play,
Mischief lurking, come what may!

My plants, they whisper thanks at night,
While I trip over toys in the twilight.
Every corner's a surprise, it's true,
Blessings wild, they're hiding from you!

Under the couch, a rogue potato,
Stashed away like a silent hero.
In every nook, a chuckle or two,
Finding joy in what's overdue!

The Art of Being Grateful

When life gives lemons, make a pie,
Or maybe a hat, oh my, oh my!
Leftover pizza, served with a laugh,
Who knew gratitude had such a craft?

A mug that says 'World's Okayest Friend',
Happiness shared, there’s no need to pretend.
Sharing the couch, remote in hand,
Grateful for snacks, isn't life grand?

Sticky notes stuck on the fridge's door,
Reminder that chaos brings joy to the floor.
Every bump in the road gets a grin,
Playing the game, let the fun begin!

Riding the wave of a life's silly ride,
Thanking the universe with arms open wide.
In the chaos of life, we’ll dance and twirl,
Gratefulness shines in this wacky whirl!

Raindrops of Kindness

Puddles splash with every bound,
Each drop a hug falling to ground.
Umbrellas that flip, hats that fly high,
Kindness showers from clouds in the sky!

Gutters giggle, puddles reflect,
Grateful for shoes that dance and connect.
Every drip whispers secrets untold,
Raindrops of kindness, brave and bold.

A rubber duck floats in the storm,
Grateful hearts finding a new form.
Dancing in rain, we stomp and play,
Brighten the gray, come what may!

When thunder chuckles and lightning winks,
We'll laugh with joy, oh how it syncs.
Raindrops fall, laughter abounds,
In every drop, a smile resounds!

Kind Words in the Silence

A whisper caught in the morning breeze,
A compliment buried under the trees.
Sunshine beaming with each breath we take,
Kind words are the magic, make no mistake!

Sneaky high-fives when no one’s around,
Winks traded softly, like love unbound.
In the quiet, giggles float,
Grateful moments, the heart's little note.

Old shoes dancing across the floor,
Kindness echoes, forever more.
A smile shared in the busy street,
Turns a stranger’s day into something sweet.

When silence hums a happy tune,
We ride the vibe, beneath the moon.
For every kindness, a chuckle or grin,
In the silence, our tales begin!

Moments of Reflection

In the chaos of the day,
I trip over my cat's play.
With a laugh and a grin,
I count my toes, not my sins.

The coffee pot goes kerplunk,
Got more grounds than any junk.
A sip and a squint, oh dear me,
Who knew beans could bring such glee?

Shiny apples on my lap,
Eat one while I take a nap.
A fruit salad for my feast,
Just don’t let the fruit fly, at least!

I look around, what a sight,
My pants fit snug, still feeling light.
In this mess, I find the cheer,
Thanks to the chaos, I hold dear.

The Warmth of Generosity

A pie sits like a globe in view,
I hope it doesn’t roll, oh who knew?
With whipped cream clouds and sugary fun,
If I share this, I might weigh a ton!

Neighbors knock with their favorite dish,
“Here’s my tuna – your wish is my wish!”
I toss them leftovers of old stew,
We’re like a charity soup, who knew?

When laughter spills like fizzy pop,
We trade our snacks, oh we can swap!
An endless bounty of jokes and pies,
With every nibble, our spirits rise.

So gather round, no need for fuss,
With silly hats and tasty crusts.
In this kitchen, love is spread,
As we dance ’round with crumbs on our head.

Kindred Souls in Harmony

Two friends and a pizza, what a dream,
Topped with laughter, and gooey cheese cream.
They argue on pineapple, what a fight,
Yet still hug it out, what a sight!

In a world of sips and sours,
We plant our joys like little flowers.
With mugs held high and tales to tell,
Even burnt toast can taste so swell!

Running through the rain, oh what fun,
Splashing puddles, on the run!
A dance-off in the downpour's glow,
Grateful for friends who steal the show.

So here’s to the ones who make us smile,
With silly antics, and funny guile.
In every joke, and every cheer,
Life’s rich moments are crystal clear.

The Heart's Bountiful Feast

A table laden—what a sight,
Gravy boats and sprightly bites!
The turkey's smiling, or so it seems,
Can’t it see us plotting teams?

Stuffing up traditions, oh what glee,
Can I eat two rolls? Or just three?
Grandma’s recipes, mixed with flair,
Like culinary hide-and-seek, beware!

Desserts set up like a parade,
Chocolate rivers, a sweet charade.
With every slice, we chant, “More please!”
From apple pie to creamy freeze.

Let's raise a toast, not just glass,
But to the moments that we amass.
In giggles and crumbs, amid the best,
We find our joy; now isn’t that blessed?

The Gift That Keeps Giving

Wrapped in paper, tied with a bow,
A gift from my friend, but what does it show?
A coffee mug shaped like a giant shoe,
At least it’s a laugh, and it’s slightly useful too.

I opened one more, what’s this surprise?
A rubber chicken? I can't believe my eyes!
Though odd and bizarre, it brings such delight,
I guess I’ll just keep it to scare off the night.

Yet every odd gift, I treasure and find,
Brings joy to my heart and tickles my mind.
Though they might be silly, they mean so much more,
Laughter's the best gift; who could ask for more?

So here’s to the gifts that make us all smile,
They’re quirky, they’re funny, they’re worth the while.
In laughter and fun, true joy we do seek,
With gifts that keep giving, the best ones are unique!

Seasons of Thankful Reflection

Leaves have fallen, brought a chill in the air,
But grandma's been knitting with love and some flair.
Her sweaters are cozy, though colors clash loud,
I wear them with pride, stand out in the crowd.

Pumpkin spice lattes in mugs that are chipped,
Just like the turkey, we laugh while it’s tipped.
The pie’s a bit burnt, oh what a great taste,
But who cares? We’re family; there’s no time to waste.

The table is full, oh what a grand feast,
With dishes and mishaps, we gather the least.
We spill and we giggle, it’s always a scene,
Grateful for laughter, and our own little team.

So here’s to the bumps on this road that we trot,
In each awkward moment, we cherish a lot.
With cheer in our hearts, and hearts open wide,
In every goofy moment, true love we abide!

Hearts Aglow with Kindness

A stray cat brought home with a meow and a purr,
His fur is a mess, but he’s fluffier than fur.
He steals all my snacks with a sly little glance,
Yet what can I say? He makes chaos a dance.

The neighbors exchanged far too many gifts,
Tons of socks, and mugs — oh, the holiday lifts!
But what tops it off is when laughter erupts,
A fine line between joy and when sarcasm cups.

With cookies that crumble and fudge that won’t set,
We feast on the mischief with no hint of fret.
As tables are crowded, we gather and jest,
True kindness means sharing—especially the rest!

So let’s raise a glass filled with fizzy delight,
To kindness in chaos and friends day and night.
For in every odd moment, we find festive cheer,
In hearts aglow, we hold our loved ones near!

Beneath the Canopy of Thanks

Under the trees, we’re having a ball,
With squirrels stealing sandwiches, oh, what a call!
The ants march like soldiers, each crumb on a quest,
Yet still here we gather, the laughter’s the best.

The bugs start their dance, a jig on our plates,
The picnics we bring are filled with odd mates.
Though ants are the guests we didn’t invite,
It’s a full-on party, the mood’s sparkling bright.

With pie and some pasta, it’s always a spread,
Even if half of it gets stuck in my head.
We giggle at mishaps as skies start to twinkle,
As love fills the air with that sweet, gooey sprinkle.

So here’s to the mess that we dance through each year,
In every blunder, we hold friendships dear.
For under the canopy, laughter resounds,
Life’s gift in the chaos and joy that abounds!

A Symphony of Appreciation

In the kitchen, pots a-clank,
With turkey dancing on the plank.
A cat in hat, a dog in socks,
Who knew feasts came with silly shocks?

Granny's jokes are quite the hit,
As cousins giggle, never quit.
Uncle's tie, a gift from last,
We raise our cups, the moments blast.

Leftovers piled, a mountain high,
We feast again, oh me, oh my!
With laughter ringing through the halls,
We'll sing our thanks, that is the call.

So here's to joy and tasty bites,
To laughter loud and silly flights.
In every silly toast we raise,
We find the joy in all our days.

Footprints of Generosity

A friend once lent me his old shoes,
They squeaked and danced, they brought me blues.
With every step, the neighbors laughed,
'Is that a turkey, or a bird who quaffed?'

I baked a pie, forgot the zest,
The pie was good, but not the best.
With whipped cream clouds all in a twirl,
They called it 'mystery'—can you unfurl?

We tripped on crumbs, made such a mess,
With giggles flying, felt so blessed.
Each stomp and spin, we thanked our fate,
For funny friends who make us great.

So wear my shoes, if you're feeling brave,
Just dance and laugh, let kindness wave.
In every mishap, find delight,
And let our joy take endless flight.

Blossoms of Thankfulness

The garden bloomed with broccoli heads,
I thought it was flowers—oh the spreads!
While butterflies danced, I made a stew,
A bit of salt, a joke or two.

The rabbits gathered, ready to feast,
I tossed them carrots; not the least!
With every crunch, a giggle rang,
Even weeds in the pot, I sang.

Neighbors peeked, with puzzled stares,
As I wore a crown of leafy wares.
In nature's bounty, we see the grace,
And every laugh, puts joy in place.

So here's to blooms, both good and strange,
To funny feasts, and moments change.
In every bite, a heartfelt cheer,
For life is silly, let's make it clear!

Threads of Heartstrings

A scarf so warm, a gift from mom,
It’s bright, it’s loose, it’s full of charm.
As I wore it, a bird flew by,
With a wink and twist, oh my, oh my!

Friends knitted warmth in a wild parade,
With yarns of laughter, the stitches played.
In every loop, a story spun,
Of holiday cheer, and quirky fun.

In every hug, there’s extra thread,
For love’s the fabric, that’s what I said.
At dinner we cheer, with turkey and pie,
Threads of fondness reach the sky.

So keep those stitches tight, my friend,
For every laugh, there’s love to mend.
In this tapestry of joy and glee,
Thankfulness flows, just let it be.

A Symphony of Grateful Hearts

In a world of clumsy gestures,
We honk and we wave our quirks.
With pies that wobble like jelly,
And smiles that cover our smirks.

The turkey's still frozen, oh dear!
We dance around with a cheer.
Fumbling forks and spilled drinks,
Yet laughter is all we can hear.

A toast with fizzy soda pop,
We hope the laughter won’t stop.
Thankful for socks that don’t match,
And every funny tale we crop.

So grab your plate, don’t be shy,
Join us for a slice of pie.
In this symphony of laughter,
Together, we reach for the sky.

Harvesting Moments of Joy

In the fields of silly antics,
We gather giggles like corn.
With potato sacks for slipping,
And marbles that were forlorn.

The dog steals the feast, what a sight!
Grandma's wig takes off in flight.
We chase laughter, not just turkey,
On a day that feels just right.

The squash does a little jig,
While cousins all do a swig.
With each smile, we plant a seed,
Of joy, we're never too big.

So gather 'round, with hearts so wide,
Let's roll in laughter, let's glide!
In the harvest of happy moments,
We dance, we play, we abide.

Threads of Connection

With threads of laughter we weave,
A tapestry no one can leave.
Found socks have become legends,
And Grandma's jokes never cleave.

The kitchen's a circus, oh dear!
Who knew that cooking would steer
Us into a flour fight frenzy,
While friends and family draw near?

We reminisce about the past,
Of mishaps that went by so fast.
Each thread of love, slightly tangled,
Reminds us of moments that last.

So here's to our quirky patchwork,
In chaos, we find our smirk.
Together, we stitch every story,
Embracing the beauty of our quirk.

A Canvas of Thanks

On the canvas of our mischief,
We paint with colors so bright.
From splatters of pie and giggles,
To joys that take flight at night.

Crayons may melt in the sun,
But our laughter cannot be done.
We'll color the world with our blunders,
Learning each day can be fun.

With handprints of memories made,
And every silly joke replayed.
Our masterpiece might seem messy,
But it's love that's beautifully laid.

So let's brush together this glee,
And embrace all that's weird and free.
In the gallery of our laughter,
We find gratitude's sweet decree.

Gifts Wrapped in Kindness

A thank you note from my pet cat,
For sharing my lunch, imagine that!
He’s grateful I feed him each day,
Though he steals from my plate, come what may.

A sweater I bought for my old goat,
He wears it with style, a real fashion quote.
He prances around in his woolly delight,
Gifts keep on giving, oh what a sight!

Thanks from the plants on my window sill,
For watered love, they grow at will.
In return, they sway and make me feel,
Their gratitude blooms, it’s quite the deal!

So here’s to the laughter, to joy in the air,
To silly moments that show we care.
With gifts that are funny and wrapped with fun,
Life's little treasures for everyone!

Luminaries of Gratitude

A glow-worm thanked me for a nice jar,
Said he'd light my way, he's a shining star.
With wiggly worms doing a jig, oh my,
They're sweet little critters who light up the sky.

The parrot squawked, 'Thanks for the treat!'
He mimics my laugh, isn't that sweet?
With feathers so bright, he revels in cheer,
Gratitude's funny when birds are near!

One dog decided to write with his paw,
'Best human ever!'—adorable flaw.
He leaves muddy prints on my floor every day,
But love's in the mess, what more can I say?

In this quirky world, a smile is found,
In gifts that are silly, joy's all around.
So let's raise a toast with laughter and glee,
To all of life's oddities, bubbly and free!

Autumn Leaves and Thankful Hearts

The squirrels scurry, collecting their loot,
Thanking me daily for the crumbs I boot.
With acorns galore and nutty delight,
Their little dances are pure, quite a sight!

Each leaf that falls gives a grateful cheer,
'We're free-falling here, isn't it clear?'
As they twirl and twist, dancing away,
They whisper their thanks in a breezy display.

The pumpkin carved smiles on my doorstep,
Grinning at neighbors, they laugh and prep.
Though rotting may come, they'll always remind,
Fun shapes and faces are a sign of the kind!

So grab an apple, take a big bite,
Share laughs with friends, make every night bright.
Gratitude giggles from nature's own art,
For joy's in the silly and warms every heart!

A Tapestry of Thanks

Weaver of quirks, stitching smirks with glee,
Every thread tells a joke, can’t you see?
A tapestry rich with laughter and jest,
Woven with warmth, certainly the best!

Oh, the socks that I gave to my old dog,
He’s dragged them around like a froggy log.
Still, he thanks me with the sloppiest kiss,
A humorous bond, hard to resist!

The garden’s a canvas where veggies conspire,
They giggle and wiggle in a vegetable choir.
'Thanks for the soil,' they cheerfully churn,
With every ripe tomato, more love we learn.

As we gather around in our mismatched chairs,
Each chuckle a blessing in our shared lairs.
Let’s celebrate antics, in humor we bask,
In this fun-filled tapestry, simply a blast!

Beneath the Canopy of Gratitude

Under a tree, we feast on pie,
Squirrels we cheer, oh my oh my!
They drop acorns, just for fun,
We laugh so hard, we nearly run.

The sky is blue, the sun's a friend,
We give high fives; there's joy to send.
Turkey trots and silly hats,
Dance like penguins, how about that?

Thank you for moments, filled with cheer,
Though the dance moves seem unclear.
With every joke, we rise and cheer,
Gratitude's here, let's spread good cheer!

So under the tree, with friends we stand,
Passing the gravy, it's really grand.
Laughter echoes, our hearts are light,
With every bite, things feel just right.

The Legacy of Kindness

A pie on the table, a cake in the air,
Someone's still missing, with a chair to spare.
We wave at the dog, who’s chasing his tail,
While Auntie sings off-key, it never gets stale.

Why do we gather, if not for the plot?
To hear Grandma’s stories, some are quite hot.
She juggles the turkey, drops it with glee,
Just like the time with the cat and the tree!

Each hug we share, a giggle ignites,
You step on a foot, and everyone fights!
But smiles soon follow, we're back in the game,
Delighted to see each unique family name.

Kindness is flung like whipped cream in air,
A legacy formed, if you really do care.
So laughter and food become our best link,
Cheers to the quirks, now let's all drink!

Canvas of Thankful Memories

With crayons and laughter, we color our past,
Making fun mischief, oh what a blast!
A splash of orange, a dash of blue,
Gratitude's canvas, painted anew.

Mom drops her spoon, the soup flies high,
Watch out for the noodles—you can't let them cry!
We giggle and wiggle, trying to help,
While Dad tells a story with great little yelp.

Each tasty bite wraps us in a hug,
Chasing the moments with a warm bug.
With friends like these, my heart's full of cheer,
Creating memories that last through the year.

So here's to the canvas, splashed and so bright,
With laughter and love, it feels just right.
Thankfulness blooms like flowers in spring,
We paint our lives, let the joy bells ring!

Sunlight After the Storm

A sprinkle of rain, then gleams of gold,
We gather around, oh the stories told!
Behind every fork, a tale does unwind,
With humor and kindness interlined.

Lit by the glow of pumpkin pie spice,
Each hiccup of laughter, oh isn't it nice?
With awkward hugs and dad jokes galore,
We challenge each other to dance on the floor!

Whiskers of joy tickle our cheeks,
In this cozy chaos, each heart speaks.
Thank you moments, wrapped tight in a bow,
Sunlight spills in, like a bright, cheerful show.

So let's raise a glass, filled with bubbly delight,
To the quirks and the laughs that make life feel right.
Through rain and through shine, together we'll roam,
With thankful hearts, in this laughter-filled home.

Floating on Thankful Breezes

A turkey tried to take a flight,
But only ended up in fright.
With stuffing dreams and gravy hopes,
He learned to waddle, not to cope.

Pumpkin pie was on the run,
It squealed, 'Oh, isn't this much fun?'
With whipped cream clouds and sugar sprinkles,
They danced and twirled, with funny crinkles.

As apples bounced, the harvest sang,
'We're all together, let joy clang!'
With every laugh and silly grin,
The feast of joy was sure to begin.

So raise a glass of fizzy cheer,
To moments shared, to those held dear.
And let the giggles fill the breeze,
In thanks for laughter, love, and ease.

A Journey of Awakened Hearts

There once was a snail, slow and wise,
Who counted his friends under starlit skies.
With shells a-shining and giggles to spare,
They'd race to the pond, in laughter, not care.

A chicken named Cluck wrote a thank you card,
But it ended up stuck, oh dear, how hard!
With feathers all fluffed and a face so red,
She learned that 'thanks' comes from the heart, not the head.

Two rabbits raced, on twitchy toes,
Spreading their thanks wherever it goes.
'You hare-larious' they would say,
As they hopped and thumped on their thankful way.

So here's to the clumsy, the goofy, the spry,
For in every mishap, our hearts can't deny.
With joy in our pockets, we'll bounce and we'll sing,
For the journey of friendship is the best kind of bling.

Emblazing Kindness

A bee with a hat held a grand debate,
'Is it honey or kindness that makes us so great?'
With flowers in bloom, they all took a stand,
And share their sweet treats across the land.

A bear found a cupcake, quite under his nose,
He tried to eat it, but soon found it froze.
In a silly jam, he began to dance,
And the forest joined in, what a wild chance!

Frogs in funny hats were croaking 'thank you,'
For bugs on a platter, a gourmet to chew!
They leaped with glee, amid giggles and croaks,
In a ribbiting rhythm, they danced like folks.

So let's shine like fireflies, bright in the night,
Sharing warmth and kindness, oh what a sight!
With laughs and a wink, let the good times flow,
For the joy of giving makes our spirits glow.

The Treasure Chest of Thank You

In a pirate's cave, a treasure was found,
But it wasn't gold – it was laughter so sound!
With 'Arrr! Thanks' and 'Yo-ho-ho!'
They shared their bounty with a silly show.

A parrot named Polly squawked from on high,
'Thank you for snacks, oh me, oh my!'
As they tossed popcorn, it flew in a swirl,
A popping parade, what a whimsical whirl.

The map to joy had a few funny bends,
With each twist and turn, more giggles ascends.
For kindness is gold, the pirates agreed,
In their treasure chest, love was the seed.

So gather 'round mates, share your good cheer,
For the funniest moments bring hearts ever near.
With thanks in our chests, like jewels they gleam,
In the adventure of life, give gratitude a beam!

Luminescence of Generosity

In the kitchen, there lies a pie,
But Grandma forgot it, oh my, oh my!
We gathered 'round, eyes wide with glee,
Expecting a feast, but got a cup of tea.

The turkey danced on the table too,
Saying, "Eat me! I'm tired of this view!"
Kids at the feast, they wave forks like swords,
Fighting for sides, it's a hilarious hoard!

Gravy spills like laughter galore,
Plates stacked high, then onto the floor.
With dogs on patrol for the crumbs that drop,
It's a festival of chaos that just won't stop!

So raise your glass to this festive plight,
For every mishap brings pure delight.
In each slip and trip, there's joy to be found,
In this glorious mess that's joyfully round!

Kindling the Fires of Thankfulness

Gather the friends with roles to play,
And which one forgot their main entree?
The casserole's missing—oh, what a shock!
But it's fine, we’ve got snacks—let’s party rock!

A toast to burnt toast, quite a special treat,
With coffee so strong, it could stand on its feet.
Uncle Joe's stories, we all know too well,
They’re like our old jokes, a funny old sell!

The kids are outside, making snowmen tall,
Except one’s still stuck in a giant snowball!
Between the laughter and the wild tales spun,
We find that together, life’s just more fun.

Here’s to the love that binds us so near,
With the moments we cherish, season to cheer.
Every blunder and slip is a gem to unearth,
In our wacky wheel of laughter, we find our worth!

A Landscape of Appreciation

On a stroll through memories shared with pride,
I trip on a shoelace; now I'm taken for a ride!
Not all roads are straight; that much is clear,
But we laugh and we roll through this wacky frontier.

Thank you for pizza, but where's the crust?
Burnt edges or none? Just give us a must!
The kids sing out, "Can we have more cake?"
And Grandma replies, "Just watch the intake!"

We craft our joy like a rustic old art,
With paint made of giggles and some doughy heart.
We hug and we tussle, as chaos unfolds,
Each moment a silly tale yet to be told.

So here's to the flops, the fumbles, the fun,
To the mishaps that happen when we come undone.
In this blend of affection, we truly see,
That laughter is the gift—the best there can be!

Stars in the Night of Gratitude

Under a sky filled with glimmering stars,
We ponder our meals, and they've left us with scars!
“Just one more slice!” echoes through the night,
But Auntie Mae’s cookies just didn’t take flight.

The dog dressed as Santa, quite a funny sight,
While Uncle Fred's snoring is the soundtrack tonight.
Around the table, with candles aglow,
We celebrate laughter in this delightful show!

With plates piled high, and a mountain of fries,
We share silly stories as time seems to fly.
Each hiccup and blunder adds spice to our tale,
In this canvas of laughter, we’re never too frail.

So let’s raise a glass to the blunders and cheers,
To nights full of laughter, and whimsical peers.
In this playful dance of awkward delight,
We’re stars shining bright in our gratitude night!

A Chorus of Appreciation

I can thank the dog, he guards my shoe,
He barks at the mailman, that's quite a view.
But when I drop food, he's quick on his feet,
In thanks for each crumb, he'll perform a feat.

The neighbor's cat, with a top hat and flair,
Gives me that look, as if life's unfair.
Yet when I have tuna, he's first in the line,
In gratitude, he prances, oh so divine.

Thankful for socks, with odd pairs they roam,
In the dryer, they dance, calling it home.
Each missing one brings a chuckle or two,
In the circus of laundry, they bid me adieu.

And though pumpkin pie steals the sweet tooth stage,
I thank the whipped cream for its curvy grace.
Together they wobble, a jiggly show,
With laughter and love, they steal the whole dough.

Seeds of Gratitude

Plant a thank you, watch it grow wide,
With roots of respect, and stems full of pride.
The squirrels will gather each acorn they find,
In a raucous applause, with their nutty behinds.

Thanking the bees for the buzz that they make,
While honing their craft, for our sweet honey cake.
“Bzzzz,” they hum, as they flit here and there,
In gratitude’s dance, without a single care.

Oh, the weather's grumpy, but I still give a cheer,
For every raindrop is a chance to revere.
Umbrellas abound with colors so bright,
A party for puddles, what a silly sight!

So let’s sprinkle thanks like confetti in air,
With laughter and joy we can share everywhere.
In every small moment, a giggle will pop,
Seeds of gratefulness never will stop.

The Light of Generosity

Here comes a pie, steaming hot from the rack,
But grandma insists, "Don't make it a snack!"
Yet when I sneak bites, she chuckles and sighs,
In the warmth of her oven, good humor will rise.

Then there's Uncle Joe with his grand tales to tell,
Of trips to the moon, or the time he fell.
Each laugh is a lantern, glowing so bright,
Illuminating hearts on a starry night.

Thanks to the cat who steals from my plate,
Her paw on my fries? Now that's just great!
With a meow of delight, she feasts on my fries,
In return for her antics, a chuckle supplies.

And friends with their quirks, all gather around,
With memories of mishaps, we're joyfully bound.
In this light of laughter, our spirits entwine,
Each moment we share is a treasure divine.

Wings of Thanks

I said thank you to the bird on a wire,
Who sings with such gusto, a musical choir.
It fluffed its soft feathers, stared right at me,
Then dropped a fine gift, oh, what fun to see!

Then there's my old bike with a squeaky old wheel,
Rolls with a wobble, but oh what a steal!
Its rusty old chain can still make me grin,
As it rattles and hums, let the fun times begin.

Each wobble a chuckle, it keeps me in tune,
Bouncing 'round corners under the moon.
Thankful for laughter that fills the night air,
With each little mishap, we dance without care.

So here's to the elves who make mischief galore,
Whisking spoons off counters, oh, what a chore!
With wings of delight, they flit to and fro,
In this chaos of joy, our gratitude grows.

The Chorus of the Grateful

In a world so bright and sunny,
We gather round, isn't this funny?
With pies and cakes stacked high and tall,
We thank the fridge for holding it all.

All the laughter, sharing cheer,
A turkey dance, let's give a cheer!
From grandma's hugs to grandpa's tales,
We're grateful for each dish that fails.

Here's to socks that match, or not,
In this feast, we're all a lot!
Gratitude flows like gravy streams,
In our hearts, we live our dreams.

With each toast, we lift our glass,
To silly moments that always last!
So let's rejoice, let spirits soar,
For crumbs and giggles, there's always more!

A Tidal Wave of Generosity

A tidal wave rolls in with glee,
Of mashed potatoes—oh, can't you see?
We thank the chefs for their fine art,
While passing rolls with a bready heart.

From neighbors who bring pie to share,
To laughing friends without a care,
With every bite, we love to cheer,
For every funny story we hear.

The cranberry sauce may jiggle so,
But our humored hearts continue to glow,
Thankfulness ties us like a bow,
In this feast where giggles overflow.

We gather close with silly tricks,
Unwrap the fun, like gift-wrapped kicks!
So wave your forks, let joy begin,
With laughter ringing, we all win!

The Dance of Giving

In the kitchen, the pots do clatter,
As we whisk and stir, with joyful chatter!
Thankful for each spice and herb,
Even when the turkey's a little disturbed.

With a salsa move, we shake the table,
A dance of thanks, we're more than able!
The veggies jump, the cake does flip,
As we celebrate with silly quips.

Raise your glass with noodle soup,
While grandma starts her funky loop.
With each funny grin, we share a hug,
All while the cat steals a quick mug.

So wear your smiles, it's quite a sight,
With grateful hearts, we dance tonight!
In every laugh, let kindness ring,
Together we make the joy take wing!

Nurturing the Spirit of Kindness

With a sprinkle here, and a dash there,
We nurture joy, like fresh cold air.
Bringing food from all around,
Where kindness blooms, our laughter's found.

From a text to say 'Howdy, friend,'
To sharing cookies that never end,
We're grateful for pants that still fit,
As we all dance, and laugh, and sit.

Pour the drinks, let stories flow,
While we avoid that broccoli show.
We toast to crumbs on our tummies round,
In this house of joy, where love abounds.

So come and gather, bring your cheer,
For our silly hearts are always near!
Together we cherish, create, and play,
In a feast of fun, we shout hooray!

Gratitude in Every Breath

I woke up this morning, what a sight!
Coffee's brewing, oh what a delight.
Thankful for socks, mismatched yet bold,
Even for that toast, which burnt in the mold.

Each hiccup of laughter, each snort that I make,
I cherish those moments, for joy's at stake.
Thankful for belly laughs, snorts in the air,
And the cat's fierce glare, like she just don't care.

Oh, the neighbor's dog, with fur like a mop,
Brings joy to my world, and never will stop.
I chuckle, I grin, for small things I see,
Like the time I tripped over that clueless bee.

So raise your glass high, to life's silly blunders,
For laughter and love, and all that it tunders.
In every small hiccup, there's joy to embrace,
Let's give a big cheer, for this wild human race!

The Palette of Appreciation

With each little canvas, in colors so bright,
I paint my day silly, and absurdly light.
Bubblegum pink for my morning toast,
And a splash of green for the cat I love most.

The coffee spills over, a masterpiece true,
Each drip and each drop, a frenzied debut.
I'll laugh at the chaos, oh what a sight,
For life is a canvas, painted day and night.

Gonna color outside the lines, just to be free,
With crayons and giggles, like a wild, crazy spree.
Let's toast our mistakes, what a colorful fuss,
Life's just a palette, humor is the plus!

So grab your bright brushes, my friend, don't be shy,
Let's splash laughter and joy, oh my, oh my!
Together we'll twirl, with no fear in our heart,
In this grand art show, we each play a part!

Ripple Effects of Kindness

Kindness is funny, like a pie in the face,
Unexpected laughter, all over the place.
You smile at a stranger and what do you find?
A wave of good vibes, it's truly one of a kind.

Step on a banana, oh, what a comic fall!
But laughter and kindness, they conquer it all.
A wink and a laugh, with a warm little shove,
Could turn your whole day into a hit from above!

Oh, take my umbrella, though clouds might be thin,
It's funny, you see, how good deeds begin.
Like catching a sneeze, or sharing a joke,
Each giggle and grin, sparks joy like a poke.

So let's make this world light and utterly bizarre,
With a dance in the rain, 'neath a whimsical star.
Spread kindness like confetti and laugh till we drop,
For joy's like a bubble – it bounces, won't stop!

Embracing the Blessings

I slipped on a banana, it’s a sight to behold,
And laughed as I stumbled, feeling quite bold.
Embrace every flop, every fumble, a treat,
For life’s little mess-ups can’t be beat!

Like finding stray socks in the dryer’s warm lair,
Each odd little chap, it's like a treasure fair.
I’ll thank all the laundry for its quirky surprise,
As I dance in the living room, laughing ‘til I cry.

A toast to the mishaps, the accidents grand,
Like the time I forgot, my sandwich was planned.
For every wrong turn leads to giggle fits,
So let’s embrace the chaos, with humor, not quits.

Raise a cheer for the flops, the laughs, and the cheer,
For life’s little quirks are what we hold dear.
In each chuckle, each wail, joy finds a way,
So let’s dance like no one’s watching today!

Milton Keynes UK
Ingram Content Group UK Ltd.
UKHW021952151124
451186UK00007B/208

9 789916 943540